Old AUCHTERARDER, BLACKFO ʼO
with ABERUTHVEN, GASK and GLE

by
Alex F. Young

Auchterarder from the south, where Ruthven Street and Montrose Street reach into the autumn countryside with its stooks of corn. From the crest of the hill, along which High Street runs, the spire of the Aytoun Hall stands out.

FURTHER READING

The books listed below were used by the author during his research. None of them are available from Stenlake Publishing Ltd. Those interested in finding out more are advised to contact their local bookshop or reference library.

Cassel's Gazetteer of Great Britain & Ireland, London, 1899.
Handbook of the Forty-fifth Annual Congress, Aberdeen, Whitsunday, 1913, SCWS, Shieldhall, Glasgow, 1913.
Kinematograph Year Book, 1948, Kinematograph Publications Ltd, London.
National & Commercial Directory of Scotland, Pigot & Co., 1837.
The New Statistical Account of Scotland, 1837.
R.V.J. Butt, *The Directory of Railway Stations*, Patrick Stephens.
Nick Haynes, *Perth & Kinross – An Illustrated Architectural Guide*, The Rutland Press, 2000.
William Maxwell, *The History of Co-operation in Scotland*, The Scottish Section of the Co-operative Union, Glasgow, 1909.
Robert Smith, *The Making of Scotland*, Canongate, 2001.
David B. Taylor (ed.), *The Third Statistical Account of Scotland*, Culross the Printers, Coupar Angus, 1979.

ACKNOWLEDGEMENTS

For their help during his research, the author wishes to thank: Colin White of Auchterarder Bowling Club; the Rev. Michael Shewan; Davie Woods; David M. McLaren; Mr & Mrs J. Butterly; Gina Somerville; Fiona Sutherland; Terry Daniels; Margaret Marquis; Michael Hally; Johannes M. Surkamp; James Docherty; Sandra Sutherland; Jack Guthrie; William C. Hutchison; Mr & Mrs Roger Brown; Jamie Roberts; Colin T. Scott-Dempster; Roy Taylor; Margaret Ellis, Gleneagles Hotel; Gillian Lonergan, The Co-operative College, Manchester; Richard Gillanders, British Geological Survey, Edinburgh; John Shaw, National Museum of Scotland; Jane Simmons, Central Library, Bedford; Jan Merchant and Steve Connolly of the A. K. Bell Library, Perth. Thanks also to Robert Grieves for contributing the photographs on pages 10, 12 and 32.

Set into the front wall of Auchterarder's Aytoun Hall, the Malcolm Fountain was gifted to the town in 1905 by Bailie Peter Malcolm (1823–1906). A bachelor, he succeeded his father's tenancy of the 60 acre Kincardine Mains Farm, which he ran with his sister Elizabeth in tandem with his business as a grain, potato and manure merchant. In an active public life he served the school board, the Trinity United Free Church, the Freemasons (Lodge St John, Auchterarder), the parish council, and the town council as a magistrate. The presentation of the granite drinking fountain marked his retiral from public life. He died on 9 October 1906.

INTRODUCTION

AUCHTERARDER

The earliest photographs in this collection come from the 1890s, but Auchterarder has a history – sometimes an unhappy one – which extends far, far, beyond the late Victorian era.

Traditionally, the seeds of the town were sown by King Malcolm III 'Ceanmor' (1031–93), who not only built a castle or hunting lodge, but granted the 'town' its 228 acre western common. However, the earliest surviving mention of Auchterarder (Gaelic – *uachdar-ard-thir* – 'upper high land') appears in a charter of 1227, in which Alexander II granted 'the teinds of the King's revenue of the lands of Auchterarder to the Convent of Inchaffray'. The name was mentioned again in a royal charter when King Robert Bruce granted a charter of land to Sir William Montifix (ancestor of the Drummond family), the then Justiciar of Scotland. Somewhere in this period it should have been granted its royal burgh status, but as it does not feature in the 1696 Rolls of Parliament it is doubtful if such status was ever granted. (However, a petition to the Convention of Royal Burghs of Scotland in 1951 resulted in the town's 'Royal' status finally being recognised.)

The first Jacobite War brought devastation. In January 1716 the Royalist army under the Duke of Argyle came to the town during their march to Perth to find that, with the exception of one house, the Jacobite Earl of Mar had burned the place down. Argyle's army spent the night in the snow, but Auchterarder's recovery was spread over many decades.

The Burgh (Police) Scotland Act, 1892, brought the town burgh status and the appointment of a provost, two bailies, honorary treasurer, Dean of Guild and six councillors to manage its affairs and its population of 2,500. The mills, particularly Hally's at Ruthven Vale, had generated employment and prosperity, but in its rural situation, agriculture was Auchterarder's main industry, with potato as the main crop, followed by cereals and raspberries.

BLACKFORD

Blackford stands in the valley of the Allan Water, south west of Auchterarder. Traditionally, its name derives from ancient times when the wife of a Caledonian chieftain drowned at the Black Ford. Water, especially spring water, has been part of the history and development of the village since. The abundance of pure spring water brought brewers and King James IV, who passed through in 1488, is said to have commented favourably on it.

Right: The fourteenth tee of the King's Course, Gleneagles, photographed around the 1920s.

Pont's map of 1601 shows the place as a hamlet and although it became a burgh of barony in 1706, it was not until the end of the eighteenth century, with building of a water powered carding mill (later a blanket weaving factory) and Tullibardine distillery, that the village begin to take shape. This growing industry meant that when the new turnpike road from Greenloaning to Auchterarder was built between 1770 and 1790 it passed through Blackford.

Distillers and brewers have come and gone but today, through Highland Spring, over 300 million litres of water from the Brae of Ogilvie are bottled and exported around the world.

BRACO

The strategic situation of Braco or Ardoch – 'high field' – was recognised by the Romans as Agricola built a fort there as part of their northern defences against the Caledonians.

However, the village only developed from land feued from James Masterton of Braco Estate in 1815 – hence its name, and not Ardoch as perhaps it should have been. The closest the village came to industrialisation was the settling of blacksmiths and farriers who serviced the farming community in the surrounding countryside, and sawmills which processed the abundant woodlands.

Aytoun Hall and its tower dominate the north side of High Street. Reporting the laying of its foundation stone on 28 March 1872, 'with Masonic honours', the *Strathearn Herald* spoke of Auchterarder perpetuating the memory of Captain Aytoun RN of Glendevon, who introduced piped water from Crook of the Moss to Auchterarder in 1833. That little is known of Aytoun may stem from this report and the journalist's assumption that all captains were of the Royal Navy. However, this was not the case. The parochial register for Kinglassie in Fife shows that Marriot Chadwick Walker Aytoun, son of Roger Aytoun, was born on 18 March 1787, and he appears in the 1841 census as a 'gentleman of independent means' living at Glendevon House, near Auchterarder. After his death in 1854 his will was recorded at Edinburgh Sheriff Court, showing him as a retired captain of the Royal Horse Artillery. The adjacent Girnal House (a girnal is a granary or storehouse) was built in the 1830s, while the Masonic Hall, at the right edge of the photograph, dates from the eighteenth century and is home to St John's No. 46.

The north side of High Street, *c*.1963. On the left, before the Star Hotel, are the premises of Morton the tailor and outfitter, while on the other side of the hotel are the Post Office, the Trustee Savings Bank, George Menzie's fishmonger's and Hogg the newsagent. On the right edge of the photograph the Crown Hotel's 'AA' sign is followed by McLaren's sweet shop, Alex Nicol's greengrocer's and Drummond the baker. The black car beyond the light coloured Hillman Minx is the 1950 Humber Hawk, registration number CMS 806, owned by Jim Docherty of Midland Coaches.

James Currie the hairdresser and tobacconist with his 'soap boy' outside his shop at No. 75 High Street in the summer of 1905. Currie lived at No. 8 Ruthven Street. His premises were rented from Thomas Fisher, a draper in Girvan, Ayrshire, and they were later taken by Charlie Bain's hairdresser's and then by 'The Venture' fruit and vegetable store before they were demolished to make a new entry to the school.

High Street photographed in 1913, with Sutherland's general store on the left before the Barony Church with its 'squat red sandstone tower'. By 1900 the original seventeenth century parish church behind the Aytoun Hall was beyond repair and a new building was planned. The architects Honeyman, Keppie & Mackintosh (Charles Rennie Mackintosh later resigned to make his own career) were commissioned and the first service in the new Parish Church was held on 8 July 1905. Beyond is St Andrew's Church, with its distinctive 80 foot tower, built between 1843 and 1845. In 1955 the congregation of this church joined with that of the West Church (since demolished) which itself was an amalgamation of the North and the South United Presbyterian churches. However, even this congregation is no more and St Andrew's is now the premises of the Gleneagles Furniture Centre.

A 1950 view of High Street, from the Co-op to the Star Hotel, where Wright's of Perth are delivering beer. On the right, the photograph spans from the premises of Peter Miller, the radio engineer, to the Royal Hotel and beyond. The town's first Co-op was the Baking Co-operative, established in 1846 and followed by the Feus Co-operative in 1860 and the Provident Co-operative in 1866. The City of Perth Society came five years later. The Baking and the Feus merged in 1920 to form Auchterarder United and was joined in 1954 by the Provident to form Auchterarder United Co-operative Society Ltd. In 1955 this joined the nationwide Scottish Co-operative Wholesale Society. The branch on the left sold hardware, while the one on the right (under the white sign board, next to Peter Miller's) sold groceries and clothing.

High Street, six years on from the previous photograph and showing the stationers A. D. Garrie & Son on the left and an Everyready van making a delivery of batteries to Peter Miller's radio shop.

A 1935 Leyland Tiger bus of James Docherty's Midland Coaches outside his home, Deansland, on High Street in the late 1940s. In 1947 Docherty took over a fleet of buses from Steven's Garage, Dunning, and started Gleneagles Coaches. However, due to the popularity of the name he later changed it to 'Midland'. Having gone from strength to strength, the firm now runs a fleet of twenty modern buses. This particular bus was scrapped in the late 1950s.

The High Street in 1963, with Mitchell's gift shop on the left and R. Watson Hogg's Cashmere Shop on the right.

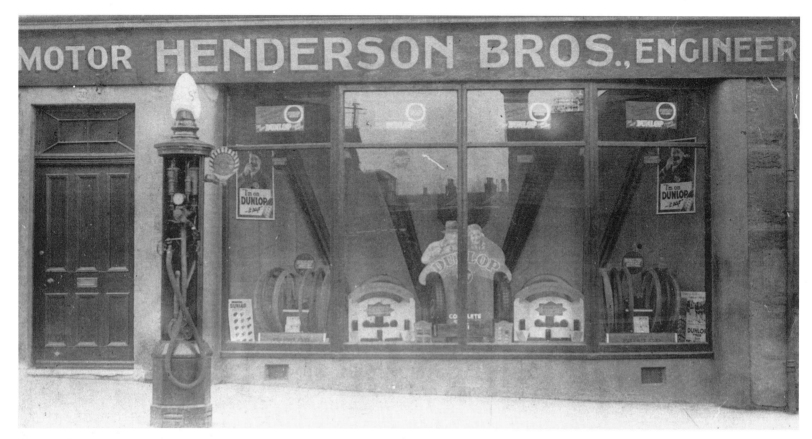

From Stirling, where his family was in the motor trade, David Henderson (or 'Snookums', when out of earshot) opened a cycle shop in Ruthven Street (now a hairdresser's) before moving to High Street in the 1920s. He continued to sell and repair pedal cycles, but expanded successively to include motor cycles, motor cars and tractors. By the early 1950s he had the only break down recovery service in the area, and, under a committee, ran the local ambulance. The roadside Shell Mex petrol pump stood at the roadside of High Street until the mid 1980s.

This view, again from 1963, moves a little further down High Street, showing a Rover car, registration number A 1000 and owned by Mr McDonald of South Kinkell Farm, coming up the hill. Past James Martin's joiner's and undertaker's workshop on the left is Henderson's Garage with the owner David Henderson standing at the petrol pump. Beyond the district nurse's black Morris Minor is the motorcycle and sidecar of Jock Stewart, the AA scout.

Standing to the south of High Street, Belvidere was built in 1849 by the Perth architect Andrew Heiton for local solicitor William Young (1798–1870), who had come to Auchterarder as an apprentice solicitor. He was also agent for the Union Bank of Scotland. Heiton returned to Auchterarder in 1855 to work on Cloan House and again in 1868 for Ochil House. Belvidere was built on the site of two earlier houses, the first dating from 1698, and this view dates from 1909. When Young's family sold the house in 1950, it passed through several owners, including a Brigadier Sanders who changed the name to Ochil Towers, before being purchased by the Camphill Movement in 1972, in whose ownership it remains. Founded in 1940, the organisation caters for children with learning difficulties and currently has a roll of thirty at Ochil.

Townhead, looking towards the town centre in 1932. On the right is the 549-seat Regal Cinema. Opened around 1927 by Peter Crerar from Crieff (where he also had cinemas), it was taken over and run by JBM Theatres of Dundee until its closure in 1963 when David Stewart, who retired to Blairgowrie, was manager. In cinema architectural terms, it was an unremarkable building. In technical terms, however, its two Kalee 8 'Indomitable' projectors, manufactured by A. Kershaw & Sons of Leeds, were, in their day, state of the art. When stripped out after closure – do you remember the last film shown? – the projectors and the cash desk were gifted to the Scottish Screen Archive at Glasgow for preservation. Externally, the building frontage consisted of a two step raised foyer, with the office on the left, a sweet shop behind the right window and a tea-room upstairs.

Townhead and the road to Stirling in the early twentieth century where the architectural change from the terrace style to the detached can be seen. The twin dormer house on the right was built in 1871.

As this 1932 photograph shows, the 'Coal Bore' with its pathways, seats and young saplings, was an attractive feature of Auchterarder's west end public park, which over the years has sadly been lost. Something of a mystery surrounds the derivation of the name 'Coal Bore'. *Cassell's Gazetteer of Great Britain & Ireland, 1899* states that 'the burgh owns about 200 acres of arable land, which was unsuccessfully bored for coal in 1873, yielding instead a splendid flow of excellent water, known as the Coalbore Springs, which have run ever since'. However, the British Geological Survey at Edinburgh has no record of such a bore and by the late nineteenth century it was well known that the Lower Devonian sandstone, upon which Auchterarder stands, would have no coal seams. The name therefore must date from an earlier period than the 1870s. In 1876 the weaving manufacturer James White applied to the Muir Commissioners to feu a portion of what was then the Beggar Muir to build a mill, utilising the bore hole water. His application came to nought and he later built his mill at Ruthven Vale.

Hunter Street, 1905. This was named after Lieutenant Colonel James Hunter of Auchterarder House. On the immediate left is the Railway Hotel, rounding the corner from High Street, and next to it the premises of John Winton the carrier.

This 1909 photograph shows the red sandstone Coll Earn House, built in the early baronial style between 1869 and 1870 to a design by the Glasgow architect William Leiper (1839–1916) for Alexander Mackintosh, a Perth born Edinburgh advocate. Leiper's later work included the Sun Life Building in Glasgow's West George Street (1889–94), which won him a silver medal at the Paris International Exhibition of 1900, and the exotic Templeton's Carpet Factory on Glasgow Green (1889–92). Little is remembered locally of Alexander Mackintosh except his daughters Dorothy and Emily, who are immortalised in stain glass windows within the house. In the 1881 census he is recorded as a fifty-nine year old widower living at Coll Earn with two servants. His home is now the welcoming Coll Earn House Hotel.

New Street, later named Montrose Street, in 1902. The street's mixture of detached and semi-detached houses, built around 1890, are unconventional as they have their gables to the road and face the open valley to Cloan House and the rising heights of the Ochils beyond. The semi-detached on the right, Wester and Easter Hassendean (named after the town in the Borders) was owned by the postmaster William F. Inglis. He lived in Wester and rented Easter to James White the weaving manufacturer. The roadway has long since been macadamised.

Built in 1875 at a cost of £2,000, Auchterarder 'Public School' accommodated 296 children and for a time ran in conjunction with the old Townhead School and the parish school at Aberuthven. A school established in 1811 by John Sheddan of Lochie, which he endowed with the interest on £1,000, conditional on teaching twelve poor children, had already been closed. The closure of the Townhead School may have necessitated the first of a number of extensions to this building, starting in 1899 with the right hand portion visible here. This photograph probably dates from the 1920s.

Auchterarder Bowling Club in 1913, with at least three of its seven rinks in play. Founded at a meeting called on Friday, 19 June 1903 by Bailie W. B. McDougall, three sites were considered: School Park, on a twenty-one year lease from the school board at £21 per annum; land between Ruthven Street and Crown Wynd; and a plot behind the post office belonging to the trustees of the late Mr James Reid. In the event, Mr Graeme Whitelaw purchased a plot in Castle Wynd from Mrs McDonald and Miss McIntosh and gifted it to the club. He became its first life member. The tenders for 'making the green' ranged from £187.10/- to £386.14.8, the latter from D. Leslie of Bishopbriggs, Glasgow, which was accepted. Working through the winter, the last piece of Cumberland turf went down on 27 January 1904 and the final cost of £617 included the green at £400, paving and drainage at £110, tools at £20, trees and shrubs at £5, and two dozen pairs of bowls, rubber mats and covers, all at £20. At the opening match on 4 June 1904, the President, Colonel John Hally of Ruthven Tower, beat the Honorary President Graeme Whitelaw 130 to 114. At the time of this photograph, the membership included three life members, sixty-seven ordinary members and two apprentices. Today the club has 120 members.

Castlebrae House in 1932. At his death in 1894, James Reid of Auchterarder House had five surviving sons – Hugh, John, Andrew and Walter, who were engineers, and Edward who studied for the ministry of the Episcopal Church. In 1897 Edward bought the land on which to build Castlebrae House for himself and St Kessog's Episcopal Church for the community. From 1921 he was Bishop of Glasgow and Galloway, and from 1931 until his death in 1938 he was Bishop of St Andrews, Dunkeld and Dunblane. Selling the house in 1970, the Reid family was followed by the Kadelski family, the Jasper family and the McDonalds before it became the Northern Police Convalescent Home in 1996.

The Roman Catholic Church of Our Lady of Perpetual Succour on Castleton Road. The Reformation Parliament of 1560 swept away Catholic churches across the country, but following the Emancipation Act of 1829 congregations again began to gather. Railway construction in the 1840s brought Irish families and Catholicism back to Scotland and congregations met wherever they could. In Auchterarder a priest came from Glasgow, and then from Crieff, once a month. On 12 May 1879 a resolution to build a chapel was passed and the site on Castleton Road was bought from Castlebrae Estate for £200. The architect was Mr G. Ewing of Muthill, while the masonry work was done by Messrs Ritchie & Son of Blackford. Other tradesmen involved were Johnstone the joiner from Perth, the local slater Eadie and the plumber McLachlan of Crieff. The building was dedicated on 5 November 1879. Since this early twentieth century photograph, a statue has been placed in the niche and the trees and curving entrance have disappeared.

The Abbey Road bridge at Ruthven Vale, where the Auchterarder to Dunning road spans the River Ruthven, in 1902. The bridge was rebuilt c.1980. To the right is Hally & Co.'s mill, built in 1878 by William Hally. William had been a middleman, supplying cottage weavers with yarn and selling the finished cloth in Glasgow, but as the industry progressed from the cottage to the mill he built a mill at Borland Park in 1850. Following the building of the sixty power-loom Castelton Mill on Castleton Road in 1863, a twenty-five loom mill was started at Ruthven Vale in 1872. In 1880 this was extended to take in the work done at Castleton and Dollerie Mill, Crieff, and by 1892 the 540 looms employed almost 400 workers to produce cloth for export markets. A major employer, during the First World War the mill produced over 100,000 yards (almost 57 miles) of army khaki. The immediate post-war period brought the beginning of the end, and the decline of the textile industry across the country. Weaving ceased here in 1956, although Gleneagles Knitwear, started in 1929, continues. Left of the bridge was the mill of Robert White & Co. White started in the cottage weaving industry in the 1840s and built a mill where Kinnoull Place now stands, moving here about 1874. A smaller concern than Hally's, it had sixty looms which produced shirting until the 1960s.

A hundred yards or so upstream (west) of the Abbey Road weaving mills, the West Mill has straddled the Ruthven for generations. It may have been a grain mill, as the 1837 *Statistical Account* of Auchterarder reports there being thirteen mills in the parish – four grain, two lint-seed oil, two flax, a saw mill, a paper mill, a fulling mill and a woollen manufactory. In living memory the mill building was a ruin although four families are recalled living in the house.

This photograph of Earnview Cottages, Auchterarder, appeared on a postcard sent in January 1917 to Mrs Gladstone of 36 Woodburn Terrace, Morningside, Edinburgh. It carried this message: 'I'm sorry I shall not be with you tonight as I am here. It's a dear old house. Granny and Grandfather are at the front. Cousin Kate and friend behind. I've had a six mile walk to Gleneagles this morning. Uncle John was here in his motor from Glasgow yesterday so we had a short three mile run. Am going out to tea in a few minutes. Will be leaving tomorrow by 8.30 a.m. train. Will see you Sunday morning or sure next Wednesday. Love to Wilma and family. From Hazel.' A trawl of records failed to identify either Granny or Grandfather.

For the Auchterarder area, the summer of 1907 saw a succession of cavalry manoeuvres and exercises as regiment after regiment came and went. This photograph, taken in the first week of July, shows part of the camp at Cloan for the 18th Hussars, the Highland Light Infantry and the Royal Field Artillery. At that time the house was owned by Richard Haldane and it wasn't every soldier who could boast of having camped in the War Secretary's garden! The exercises were also a social event and among the guests at Cloan that week were Major General Douglas Haig, at that time Director of Military Training, and Winston Churchill, Under Secretary of State for the Colonies.

The south entry to Aberuthven in 1897, with one of the blacksmiths, perhaps David Henderson or Peter Stalker, whose premises were out of shot on the right, passing the time of day with the two men, one of whom would have been the joiner Peter McEwen, who rented the house on the right from his employer, Peter Kaye, a beamer of Perth. Their dress suggests that it was a Sunday. The heap of stone chips opposite, is road metal for repairs or remaking. The macadamised roads had yet to be tarred.

The top of Aberuthven, looking to the trees around the manse and the road to Perth, photographed in 1908.

A cottage nestling among the trees in the wooded Kincardine Glen, to the south of Auchterarder, in the summer of 1913.

Situated off the road through Glen Eagles, the white harled Gleneagles House was built in the 1750s by the Haldane family who also had (unfulfilled) plans for a Palladian mansion. This 1909 photograph also shows the avenue of lime trees planted to commemorate the Battle of Camperdown (Kamperduin), where, on 11 October 1797, the Dutch fleet, under Admiral de Winter, was routed by a British fleet under the command of Admiral Adam Duncan (1731–1804). Because of their defeat, the Dutch were unable to assist in the Irish Rebellion the following year.

A fleet of buses owned by Walter Alexander of Falkirk arrive at Gleneagles Hotel in the early 1930s. This was the era of the 'Grand Hotels' built by the railway companies on the concept that 'guests will travel on our trains, to our hotels, to play on our golf courses' (Turnberry in Ayrshire was another example). While holidaying in Strathearn around 1910, Donald Matheson, general manager of the Caledonian Railway Company, recognised the potential of the land of White Muir of Auchterarder for such a hotel and in 1913 founded Gleneagles Ltd to build it and a rail link from Crieff Junction. Stopped for the First World War, building work resumed in 1922 and what the press dubbed 'The Playground of the Gods' opened in June 1924. Through the '20s and '30s the hotel became the holiday venue for high society and for wealthy Americans and its future reputation was made.

A trio of golfers on the ninth tee – the Westlin' Wyne – of the Queen's Course at Gleneagles in 1920. As the golf courses (the King's and the Queen's) were to be the hotel's *raison d'etre*, James Braid, five times winner of the British Open Championship between 1901 and 1910, but who had since turned to golf course design, was commissioned. Both courses were completed and being played over by 1918. A 491 yard, par 5 hole, the tee shot on the Westlin' Wyne should be played down the right side of the fairway to open up the remainder of the hole, and the second played straight at the flag. Good luck!

In case of the (unusual) event of a guest at Gleneagles not being a golfer, tennis courts were laid out in the grounds. Since the mid 1980s other interests catered for include clay pigeon shooting, falconry, fishing, horse riding and off-road driving.

Blackford viewed from Kirk Brae in 1910. The railway station opened for services on 22 May 1848 on the completion of the Stirling to Perth line by the Scottish Central Railway. It closed on 11 June 1956 and Mr William Duthie was the last stationmaster. The line still operates, although the buildings, with the exception of the stationmaster's house-cum-ticket office, are gone. In the right middle distance, with its distinctive roof vents, is the brewery and maltings erected by W. B. Thomson Ltd from 1886. The company also produced aerated waters, but in the early 1900s when brewing suffered a slump, the 'soft' and the 'hard' sides of the business were separated. John Craik & Co. of Perth bought the aerated water business and brewing ceased in 1915. In 1931 Veda Bread leased the maltings and they remain in the company's possession.

Blackford's southern approach along Moray Street (named after the local laird, Moray of Abercairney) photographed in 1899 with the Moray Arms Hotel (now converted into flats) on the left and the Norman style Parish Church (built 1850) on the right. Further along on the right was the Free Church, built in 1855–56 in the wake of the 1843 Disruption, but now the workshop of the blacksmith, John Hally. On Thursday 9 April 1914 this spire on the Free Church was shattered by lightning and the falling masonry killed Archibald Sinclair, an eighty-three year old retired estate contractor, who lived next door.

Moray Street, from the west end, in 1899. At that time the Blackford Hotel (currently the Coaching Inn) on the Joiner's Close corner, would indeed have been a coaching inn, serving carriages on the main Stirling to Perth road (now the A9 by-pass which was completed in 1982). The building beyond, with the dormer windows, was the 'Barracks' (now Blackford House), and next to it is the arched entrance to what was then W. B. Thomson's brewery.

Stirling Street, which pre-dates the parallel Moray Street, around 1909, with a family outside their home in Anderson's Building on the right.

Dominating the south end of the village is the war memorial erected in 1922, after the roadway was realigned, to commemorate the twenty-six Blackford men who lost their lives in the First World War while serving with, among other regiments, the Black Watch, the Royal Scots, the Gordon Highlanders and the Highland Light Infantry. The photograph dates from the summer of 1939, just before the war which would add a further twelve names to the memorial.

An elderly man and a young woman stand at the main entrance to Ardoch House, between Ardoch Bridge and Lindum, the Roman Camp, in the early twentieth century. North Lodge, or Scobie's Lodge as it was known, is on the right. Whether the man was the gamekeeper, or perhaps the estate gardener, and the woman his daughter, is not known. They may have been Mr Scobie and Miss Scobie.

Braco viewed from the north, looking across Feddal Road to the tower of the old Free Church, the graveyard, the lines of the houses in Church Street and Front Street and the Ochil Hills on the horizon. Built in 1844, following the Disruption, the Free Church had a spire until it was struck by lightning in June 1874. The repair work left a tower, which survived the demolition of the church in 1920. Since 1950, when this photograph was taken, the foreground has given way to housing.

The open ground to the right of this view of Front Street now holds the war memorial and the houses of Gentlecroft. For a time it was used as the site of the local agricultural show.

Church Street, looking north to Feddal Road, on a sunny winter's day early in the twentieth century. On the left, at the junction, is the United Free Church. At the Disruption in 1843, the Rev. Samuel Grant and part of the established church congregation seceded to found Braco Free Church. Work started on their new church in 1844 and it was consecrated on 5 January 1845. In 1900, when the Free Church joined the United Presbyterians, this building became redundant and was demolished in the 1920s.

A wintry day in Feddal Road in the early 1900s with children either running to or from the school, which stands on the left with the headmaster's house. The school could accommodate 153 children, although the average attendance was at that time less than half this figure. Typical of rural districts at this period, where so many children were from farms, the farming calendar dictated their school attendance. Beyond the Bog Green, on the right, was the parish church manse, then occupied by the Rev. George McNaughton.

Standing off the Crieff road, two miles north of Braco, the original Old House of Orchill was home to the Grahams, the family of the Dukes of Montrose. This 1897 photograph, with the lake and boathouse (which survives) in the foreground, shows the 'new' Orchill House, built in 1868 by the Perth architect Andrew Heiton (1823–94) for the Rev. John McDougall of Dundee who had purchased the estate the previous year. In 1888 it was bought by Sir Samuel Smith (1836–1906), Liberal MP for Flintshire. This photograph was taken in 1898. Following Smith's death, the Rev. Thomas Crawford became the new owner, but his home suffered a devastating fire in 1917 which caused partial destruction. The damage was made good, but as the twentieth century progressed a state of decrepitude increased throughout the house. Only since the coming of the present owners in 1995 has a serious programme of restoration been undertaken.

Dating from the sixteenth century, when it was a square tower or keep, Braco Castle was owned by the Earls of Montrose (promoted from dukedom) until the end of the eighteenth century. It was garrisoned by the Earl of Mar's Jacobite army before the Battle of Sheriffmuir on 13 November 1715. Over the years many additions and extensions were made, including one for a hoped for, but not fulfilled, visit by King George III. This photograph was taken in 1898.

Built by John Home Drummond on the north bank of the River Earn, close by Kinkell Bridge, between 1821 and 1835, Millearne House was demolished in 1969. Only the stable court remains, along with a Puginesque cross which was erected in 1840 to commemorate Drummond's mother, Janet Jardine.

The neo-classical Gask House was built on the rising ground north of the River Earn between 1801 and 1805. It was designed by the architect Richard Crichton (1771–1817), who had worked with the Adam brothers, for the Jacobite laird, Laurence Oliphant. Following the Battle of Culloden Oliphant had fled to France for sixteen years of exile. Of his three children, Charles, Charlotte and Carolina, we have the latter to thank for the songs 'Will ye no' come back again', 'The Land o' the Leal', and 'The Rowan Tree'. She died at Gask House in 1845. This photograph shows the house in 1913.

Built of local red sandstone in 1832 by the Edinburgh architect William Burn (1789–1870) for Lieutenant Colonel James Hunter, Auchterarder House epitomised Burn's Jacobean style. Major Patrick Hunter succeeded to the estate in 1874 and in 1887 he sold it to James Reid, the locomotive manufacturer of Hyde Park Locomotive Works, Glasgow. Among the additions made by Reid was the West Lodge at the main entrance. This photograph dates from 1909. For a number of years it was the seventeen bedroom Auchterarder House Hotel, but the building is now once again a private dwelling.

Born in Kilmaurs, Ayrshire, in 1823, James Reid was apprenticed to a local blacksmith before setting off to seek his fortune, firstly in Greenock, where he became chief draughtsman with the engineers Caird & Co. At the age of thirty he became manager of the Hyde Park Locomotive Works, then at Anderston in Glasgow, and after a spell with Sharp, Stewart & Co., the locomotive builders at Manchester, he returned to Glasgow to become manager of the Springburn Locomotive Works. Thoughts of retiral may have prompted the move to Auchterarder House in 1887, when he was sixty-four, but he merely took up new tasks. In Glasgow he had been a town councillor, Dean of Guild, served on Springburn School Board, and was president to both the Society of Engineers and Shipbuilders and the Royal Glasgow Institute of Fine Arts. In Auchterarder he was chairman of the Muir Commission, the local Conservative Association and the Parochial Board. Recreational organisation in Auchterarder, including the curling club and the golf club, also benefited from his munificence. This statue of Reid in Springburn Park, Glasgow, was sculpted by Sir William Goscombe John and unveiled on 3 October 1903.